بسم الله الرحمن الرحيم

SACRED
KNOWLEDGE
FOR KIDS

www.facebook.com/sacredknowledgeforkids

Prolance

www.prolancewriting.com
California, USA
©2019 Ameena bint Abdir Rahman
Illustrations ©2019 Reyhana Ismail

ISBN: 978-1-7338267-1-6

PURITY & PRAYER

A RHYMING PICTURE BOOK OF SACRED RULINGS

WRITTEN BY AMEENA BINT ABDIR RAHMAN

ILLUSTRATED BY REYHANA ISMAIL

FIQH SUPERVISED BY IMĀM TAHIR ANWAR & USTADHA SHAMIRA CHOTHIA AHMED

EDITED BY HOSAI MOJADDIDI

PROLANCE

رَبِّ اجْعَلْنِي مُقِيمَ الصَّلَاةِ وَمِنْ ذُرِّيَّتِي رَبَّنَا وَتَقَبَّلْ دُعَاءِ

Du'a of Ibrahīm عليه السلام 14:40

Rabbij'alni muqeema salaati wa min dhurriyyati, rabbana wataqabbal dua'a.

O my Lord, make me one who establishes regular prayer and also raise such among my offspring, O our Lord! And accept Thou my prayer!

This book is meant to be a delight to the ear and eye.
If you and your child find joy in reading it,
to Allah belongs all Praise.

Kindly note this book does not teach
how to pray,
but the *rulings* of prayer.

It can be used as a tool
once a child is firm in their practice
of *wudu* and prayer with all the *sunnahs*.

بِسْمِ اللهِ الرَّحْمَنِ الرَّحِيمِ
PREFACE

This collection of rhymes on purity and prayer is meant as a fun introduction to key concepts of *fiqh* before the age of accountability. There is an Appendix in the back to help guide the parent, however it is always best to study with a qualified teacher.

The poems that follow are not a substitute for a full *fiqh* text. Mature concepts are not covered. They do contain basic minimum requirements for validity of prayer in accordance with the Hanafi *madhhab*:
- *Fard* of *wudu*
- Breakers of *wudu*
- Basics of *tahara*
- *Fard* of prayer
- *Wajib* of prayer
- Prostration of forgetfulness
- Breakers of prayer

The three introductory poems aim to convey the following in an age appropriate way:
- We can call upon Allah ﷻ in any state (*du'a*)
- In order to stand before Allah ﷻ, we need to prepare ourselves (*salah*)
- Some reasons we pray and where we learned the rules of prayer (*fiqh*)

We pray Allah ﷻ grants us sincerity, accepts this work, and makes it a source of enjoyment and guidance for our children. Amīn.

AUTHOR'S NOTE

Assalaamu Alaikum wa Rahmatullahi wa Barakathu.

Dearest Parents and Teachers,

Like many Muslims, I learned the basics of *fiqh* as an adult. *Alhamdulillah*, I am fortunate that I live in an area rich with qualified teachers. After studying with Imām Tahir Anwar and Ustadha Shamira Chothia Ahmed, I was excited to pass on what I had learned to young children so perhaps they would get a head start in the knowledge that I didn't.

In the summer of 2012, I was invited to teach a group of young girls the basics of purity and prayer. Knowing the girls, the youngest of whom was 6 years old, would not enjoy *fiqh* as it was traditionally taught, I composed several short poems based upon *The Absolute Essentials of Islam*, compiled by Shaykh Faraz Fareed Rabbani. I began with the *fard*, *wajib* and breakers of prayer. As always, Imām Tahir was there for me from the very beginning, offering encouraging words and checking my work. May Allah ﷻ be pleased with him. Amīn.

For the *wajib* of prayer, I decided to make the rulings easier to remember by putting them into three distinct categories: what you say, how you recite and postures of prayer.

The poems were not meant for serious study, but as a fun introduction to *fiqh* concepts. I supplemented the poems with handouts, discussions and in later classes, crafts. *Fiqh* can be a dry subject, but the girls seemed to actually enjoy reading the poems aloud in class. The rhyme also made the material easy to memorize for those who wished to do so.

Later I added the *fard* of *wudu* and breakers of *wudu* from *The Absolute Essentials of Islam*. To make the poems well-rounded, I decided to add the prostration of forgetfulness and basics of *tahara* which I compiled from two other texts: *Nur al Idah* and *Ascent to Felicity*.

After completion of the poems, it was Ustadha Shamira who encouraged me to compile an Appendix so that others might use the poems to teach. This was a far more intimidating project, but the Appendix was finally completed in 2017. May Allah ﷻ be pleased with Ustadha Shamira, and accept it from her. Amīn.

When the poems were complete but the Appendix was still in progress, I invited sisters from the community who were mothers or spiritual mothers for feedback. I did my best to listen and incorporate their ideas on how to improve the work. May Allah ﷻ bless them all. Amīn. One of the comments was that the poems lacked spirituality. This was actually purposefully done as I didn't want the *fiqh* rulings to be confused with other ideas. However, taking the idea to heart, I wrote 3 new poems which described: *du'a*, *salah*, and some reasons why we pray. By this time the *fiqh* poem illustrations were complete. To make these new illustrations a little different, we decided to center them around the three great mosques as an introduction to the book.

I worked with Sister Reyhana Ismail, our illustrator, for almost 2 years. The vision was to create colorful, joyous, dynamic scenes. This was challenging as the poems were not a story, but lessons in *fiqh*. After consulting others, I decided on scenes of children in everyday situations having fun, but making *wudu* and/or praying. I didn't want the illustrations to look like a textbook. Sister Reyhana did a beautiful job *masha Allah*. May Allah ﷻ be pleased with her. Amīn.

Though I have studied *fiqh*, I am not an *'alimah*. The aspects of *fiqh* have been checked for accuracy by my *fiqh* teachers Imām Tahir and Ustadha Shamira. May Allah ﷻ bless them for their generosity with their time. Over a period of years, they spent many hours reviewing the poems paragraph by paragraph via email, and thereafter the Appendix via email and once again on paper.

I did strive for excellence and I kindly ask forgiveness for any shortcomings in this work. Any good has been from Allah ﷻ and any mistakes have been my own. I pray it is of benefit to this *Ummah*.

Due to their "*fiqh*" nature, please do not alter the poems, as they are considered accurate and complete as is. Instead, I encourage you to contact me via Sacred Knowledge for Kids with suggestions for improvements.

I humbly request your *du'as* for acceptance by Allah ﷻ, and kindly request *du'as* for my teachers, without whom I would be lost.

Jazakum'Allahu khayran.

Wasalaam,

Ameena bint Abdir Rahman (Umm Qaasim)

www.sacredknowledgeforkids.com/contact.html

DU'A AND SALAH

بسم الله الرحمن الرحيم

THE PROTECTING FRIEND

Allah is your Protecting Friend
You can call on Him again and again.

When you're tired or you're at ease,
You can make *du'a* any time you please.

Day or night it is your choice,
It pleases Him to hear your voice.

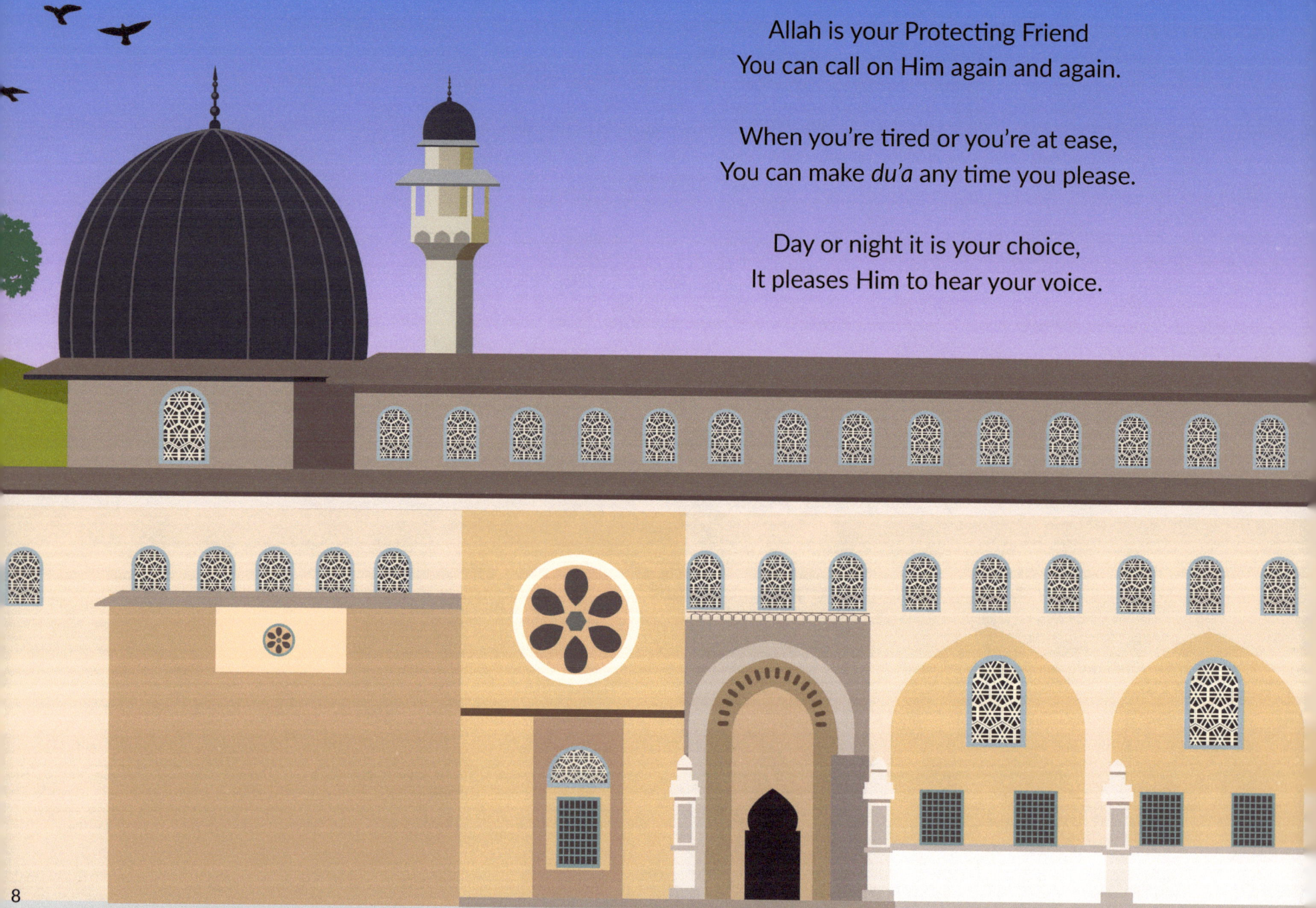

You can talk to Allah about your day.
You can ask Him to take your pain away.

When you're happy or when you're scared,
Your Protecting Friend is always there.

In your pajamas or in your best clothes,
After gym class, or smelling like a rose.

Ask Allah silently or ask out loud,
When you're all alone, or in a crowd.

The line is open for you to say,
What's in your heart, night or day.

Du'a is almost like making a call,
You don't have to prepare anything at all!

THE KING OF KINGS

Prayer is different than making *du'a*,
Prayer is like we're visiting Allah.

Even when we visit a friend,
We go the time they say to attend.

We wear good clothes and comb our hair.
Go all dirty? We would not dare!

We follow directions to get to their house,
For if we don't we will get lost!

We have good manners when we're there,
Ignoring them would not be fair.

So when we visit The King of Kings,
We keep in mind all these things.

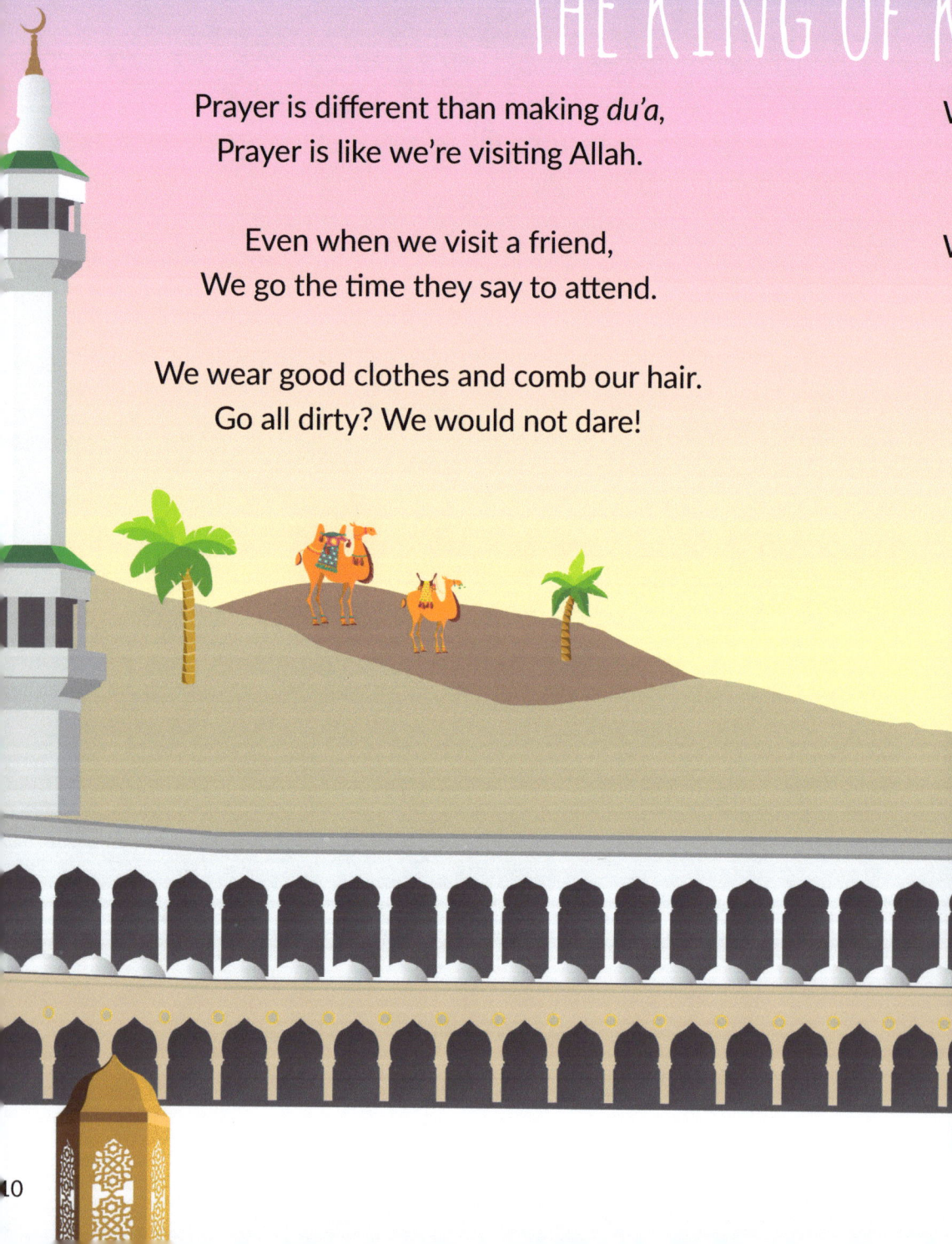

We go the times He invites us in.
We can't be late if we want to win.

We groom ourselves the way He taught,
About what is right and what is not.

We follow our beloved *Nabi*'s directions,
For his worship was complete perfection.

We try to do everything just right,
As Allah's guests we're more than polite.

Such an awesome thing to pray
And be with Allah five times a day!

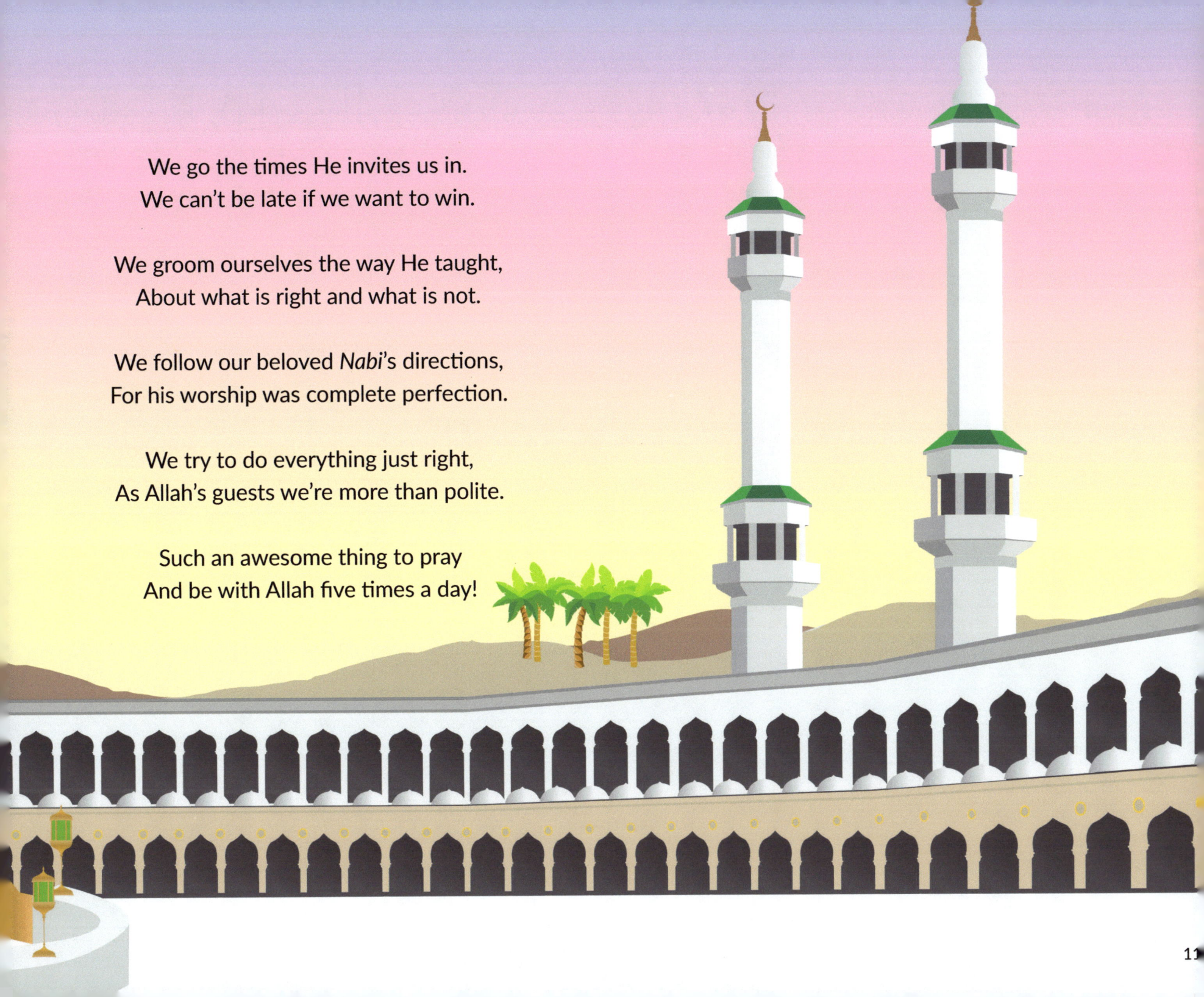

THE GENTLE, THE FORGIVING

Allah is Gentle and He draws us near
And because we love Him, we love to appear

At His door to help remind us
Of all His gifts and all His kindness.

Our *salah* reminds us to be good
The way that every Muslim should.

Our Prophet said that prayer is light
A light that shows us wrong from right.

A calming light that guides our way,
So our path is straight, and not astray.

Prayer will give you extra power,
It protects your heart like a castle tower.

So learn your *salah*, and do your best
To make your prayer a time for rest.

Allah, His *Rasool*, and our blessed scholars
Have special guidelines that they have taught us

About purity and prayer contained in this book.
So just relax, and take a look!

We made them rhyme so you'll have fun,
And you'll be wiser when you're done!

Then be with Allah, The Gentle, The Forgiving
And thank Him for the life you are living.

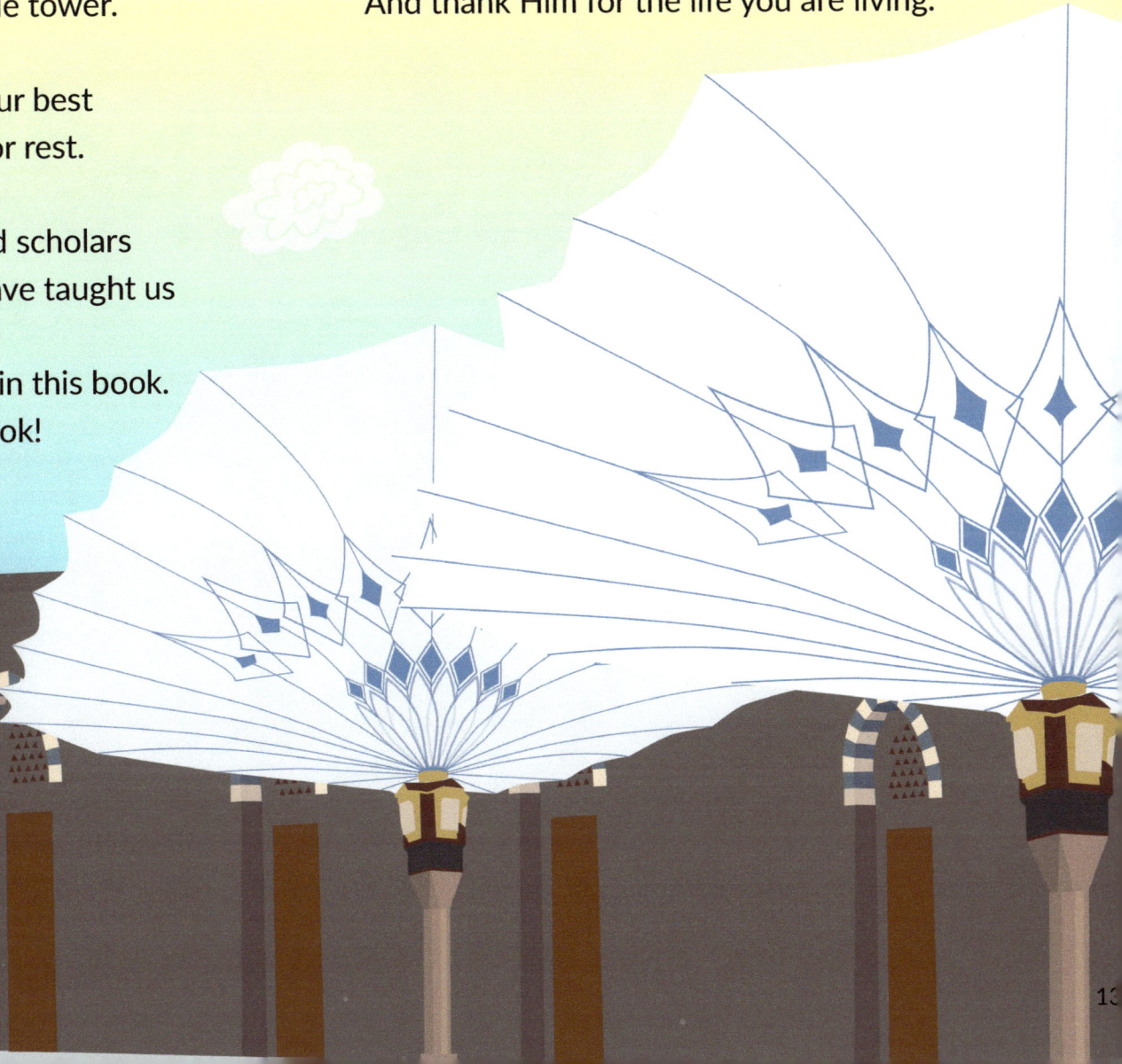

PURITY

بسم الله الرحمن الرحيم

FARD ACTS OF WUDU

Three parts to wash, and one part to wipe. And they are each of a different type.

The one part you wipe, is your head
So don't try to wash your head instead!

Face, arms, and feet - it is very true
You must wash them to make *wudu*.

When you wash, here is the difference:
The water must drip in this instance.

First face, then arms, then head, then feet.
The *fard* of *wudu* are now complete.

To wash your face, all must be wet
Do it right and you're all set.

From top of forehead, to bottom of chin
Do it right, and you will win.

From one earlobe to the other
Tell your sister and your brother.

If all is wet, then all is good
You did it like the Prophet would!

Wash hands and arms, all must be wet
Do it right and you're all set.

Include your elbow, it must be wet
Do it right and you're all set.

A fourth of your head above the ears
Is what you wipe so have no fears!

Include the ankles when you wash your feet
Now all the essentials are complete.

ACTIONS THAT BREAK WUDU

Know there are things that break your *wudu*,
Like when *najasa* or air comes out of you!

Every time this happens to you,
Please make sure to repeat your *wudu*!

When you're praying you're talking to Allah,
Laughing quietly will break your *salah*.

But while you're praying it is also true,
Laughing aloud will break your *wudu*!

Wudu puts you in a purified state.
You know what's happening when you're awake,

But if you happen to lie down to sleep,
Repeat your *wudu* your state to keep.

WATER

If you make your *wudu* in a beautiful way,
The Prophet will know you on Judgment Day.
Your limbs will shine and he will know,
It's because of *wudu* your face does glow!

If you have very little water,
Whether you're a son, or a daughter,
Your face, your arms, your head, your feet,
The *fard* of *wudu* are now complete.

If the *fard* are done in a perfect way,
To Allah Most High, now you can pray.
If you miss your face, arms, head, or feet,
Then your *wudu* is not complete!

But if you know you have enough water,
Whether you're a son, or a daughter,
Then of course it's nothing new,
You should do a complete *wudu*.

WASHING

There are some things that stick to your skin,
The water just rolls and can't get in.
If this ever happens to you,
Please clean it off before making *wudu*!

If some *najasa* gets onto you,
You truly don't have to repeat your *wudu*!
Just wash it off, up to three times,
Aren't you glad this lesson rhymes?

If *najasa* is there, but you can't really see,
Then you must always wash it times three!
After you do, there's no need to doubt,
That all the *najasa* is already out.

In the washroom you take care of your need,
Wipe, wash, wipe is best indeed.
In the washroom you take care of your need,
Wearing slippers is best indeed.

PRAYER

بسم الله الرحمن الرحيم

FARD: CONDITIONS BEFORE PRAYER

Before I can even start to pray
I have to be sure it's the right time of day.

Purify my body, my clothes, and my space,
Girls cover all except hands, feet, and face.

But for the boys, it happens to be
Right below the navel to right below the knee.

Toward the qiblah I turn my chest and heart
I make the intention to pray before I start.

I stand and say "*Allahu Akbar*" — Allah is the Greatest!

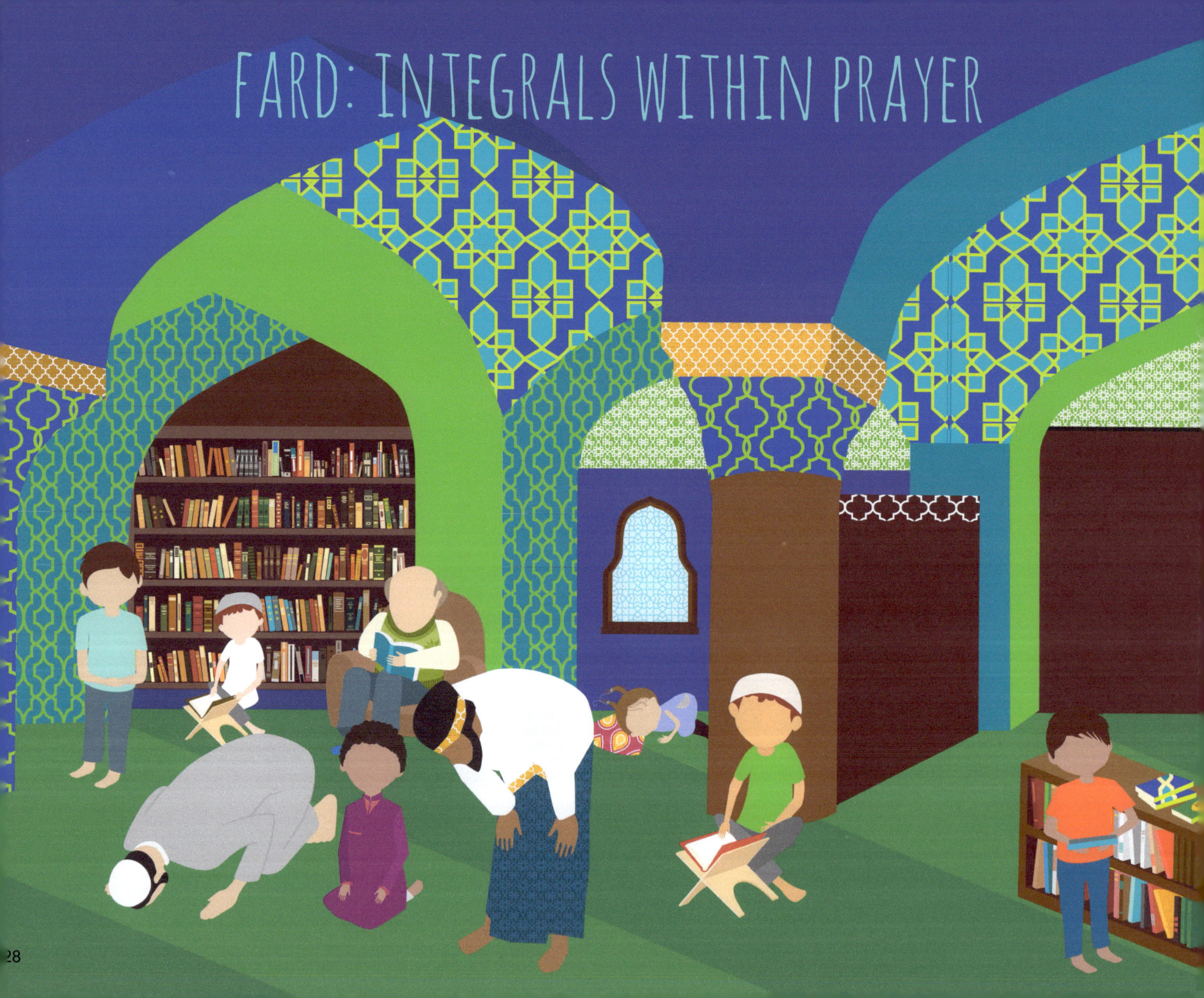

FARD: INTEGRALS WITHIN PRAYER

Now we come
to the bones of the prayer
But it is only the very first layer.

If you forget any of these,
Repeat the entire prayer please!

All of us must stand, and I truly can.
I must recite one verse of Qur'an
but I do not recite it behind the imām!

I must bow to the Lord of the Worlds
I must prostrate to the Maker of boys
and girls.

I must sit at the final sitting
As long as *tashahhud* to do
Allah's bidding.

If you forget any of these,
Repeat the entire prayer please!

WAJIB: WHAT YOU SAY

Now we come to the flesh of the prayer
But it is only the second layer.

If you forget any of these,
Do a special prostration please!

There are things that you say, and things that you do.
And the way that you do them is important too.

For a *fard* prayer, these are the rules.
For a *fard* prayer, these are the tools.

Al Fatiha is one of the *surahs* you say
In the first 2 *rak'ahs* recite it when you pray.

A *surah* or 3 verses is also what you say
In the first 2 *rak'ahs* recite it when you pray.

WAJIB: WHAT YOU SAY 2

For *sunnah* and *Witr*, these are the rules.
For *sunnah* and *Witr*, these are the tools.

Al Fatiha is one of the *surahs* you say
In EVERY *rak'ah*, recite it when you pray.

A *surah* or 3 verses is also what you say
In EVERY *rak'ah*, recite it when you pray.

In the second and last *rak'ah*
Sit and say *tashahhud* for Allah.

Remember when you're praying your *salah*
You are really talking to Allah.

And say two *salām* when your prayers end
To people, the imām, and angels intend.

If you forget any of these,
Do a special prostration please!

WAJIB: HOW YOU RECITE

How you recite is something you do
How you recite is important too.

To recite aloud means others can hear
When you do your prayers you have nothing to fear.
To recite quietly means only you can hear
When you do your prayers you have nothing to fear.

In *Fajr, Maghrib, 'Isha*: Qur'an is recited aloud
By the imām only and not the crowd (followers).

And for all five prayers behind the imām
You recite everything except the Qur'an.

A girl recites quietly when praying alone
Allah made it easy for her to pray at home.

For *Fajr, Maghrib, 'Isha*: boys have a choice
To recite in a loud or quiet voice.

The choice is when they're praying alone
But the *masjid* is better than praying at home.

If you forget any of these,
Do a special prostration please!

WAJIB: POSTURES OF PRAYER

The postures of prayer are something you do.
The postures of prayer are important too.

Make two prostrations in each *rak'ah*.
In prostration, you're closest to Allah.

Between your prostrations, for a moment be still.
To be calm and peaceful is Allah's will.

After you bow, for a moment be still.
To be calm and peaceful is Allah's will.

THERE IS ONLY
ONE WAY
TO
SUCCESS
★ IT'S CALLED ★
HARD
WORK

IF YOU CAN'T DO
GREAT
THINGS,
DO SMALL THINGS
IN A
GREAT
WAY.

You should sit in the second *rak'ah*
Allah will ask you about your *salah*.

How long should your sitting be?
The length of *tashahhud* for you and me.

If you forget any of these
Do a special prostration please!

THE PROSTRATION OF FORGETFULNESS

How do you do the special prostration?
I will give you an explanation!

You do it all at the final sitting
First say *tashahhud* from the beginning.

One *salām* to the right, then 2 prostrations
Is the shortest explanation!

After the prostrations you remain sitting
Then again start *tashahhud* from the
beginning.

Then as always, *durood* and *du'a*
Ending with *salāms* completes the *salah*.

Now that you know it, *alhamdulillah*
Now you can do it, *masha Allah*.

ACTIONS THAT BREAK THE PRAYER

Know there are things that break your *salah*,
So have good manners when you pray to Allah.

If you do any of these,
Start your prayer over please!

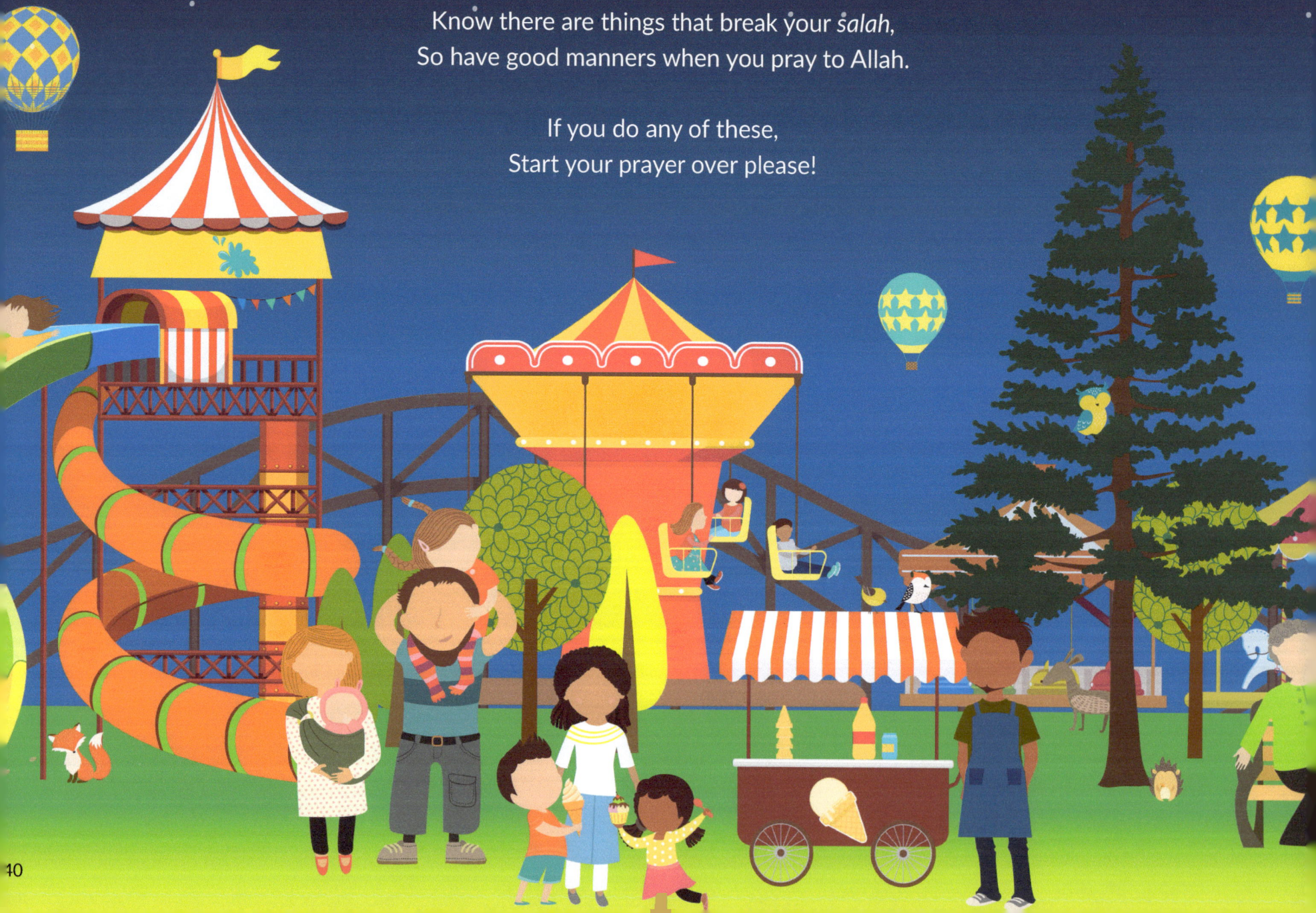

Your only movement should be the prayer,
Moving too much means you don't care!

You shouldn't talk, you shouldn't eat,
The King of Kings is the one you meet.

Do not moan and do not cry,
Keep your heart with Allah Most High.

Do not cough (without need), or change direction,
You are under Allah's protection.

Recite by heart and not a book
The place of *sajda* is where you look.

Recite correctly with all your heart
Allah and you will never part.

THE BOOK OF THE REMEMBRANCE OF ALLAH

Mu'adh ؓ reported:
The Messenger of Allah ﷺ took hold of my hand and said,
"O Mu'adh! By Allah I love you, so I advise you to never forget
to recite after every prayer:

'Allahumma a'inni ala dhikrika, wa shukrika, wa husni 'ibadatika

(O Allah, help me remember You, to be grateful to You,

and to worship You in an excellent manner).'"

[Abu Dawud]

وَعَنْ مُعَاذٍ رَضِيَ اللهُ عَنْهُ أَنَّ رَسُولَ اللهِ صَلَّى اللهُ عَلَيْهِ وَسَلَّمَ أَخَذَ بِيَدِهِ وَقَالَ: "يَا مُعَاذُ وَاللهِ إِنِّي لَأُحِبُّكَ" فَقَالَ: "أُوصِيكَ يَا مُعَاذُ لَا تَدَعَنَّ فِي دُبُرِ كُلِّ صَلَاةٍ تَقُولُ: اللَّهُمَّ أَعِنِّي عَلَى ذِكْرِكَ، وَشُكْرِكَ، وَحُسْنِ عِبَادَتِكَ . رَوَاهُ أَبُو دَاوُدُ بِإِسْنَادٍ صَحِيحٍ

APPENDIX

بسم الله الرحمن الرحيم

RULINGS OF SACRED LAW

Quoted directly from *Absolute Essentials of Islam* compiled by Shaykh Faraz Fareed Rabbani, based on Shaykh Amin Jundi's *Islah 'Ilm al-Hal* (with permission of Shaykh Faraz)

In the Hanafi school, the actions of those morally responsible take one of eight rulings:

1. The obligatory (*fard*) is a firm command established by a decisively established text whose meaning is decisive and not open to the possibility of interpretation.

One is bound to believe in and act on the obligatory. The one who denies it could well fall into disbelief, and the one who leaves it is sinful.

If an obligatory element of an action is omitted, the action remains unfulfilled. Thus if one omits an obligatory act of the prayer (such as a condition or integral), the prayer is invalid and unperformed.

2. The necessary (*wajib*) is a firm command supported by a text that allows for the possibility of interpretation.

Denying something necessary is corruption (*fisq*), not disbelief. Leaving it is sinful.

The omission of necessary elements of the prayer does not nullify one's prayer. However, it becomes necessary to repeat one's prayer if some necessary element was omitted intentionally. If omitted absentmindedly, forgetfulness prostrations are necessary (*wajib*) at the end of the prayer. If these too were left out, then it is necessary (*wajib*) upon one to repeat one's prayer.

3. The emphasized *sunnah* (*sunnah mu'akkada*) is that which our Prophet ﷺ or Companions did most of the time and was not of worldly habits.

Leaving an emphasized *sunnah* is blameworthy but not sinful. Habitually leaving such a *sunnah*, however is sinful, because it entails "turning away" from the guidance of the Messenger of

Allah ﷻ, whom we have been commanded to follow.

4. The recommended (*mustahab*) is that which our Prophet ﷺ did sometimes, or was of his worldly habits.

Performing the recommended is rewarded, but leaving it is not sinful or blameworthy.

5. The permissible (*mubāh*) in itself is neither rewarded nor punished. Such acts are rewarded, however, if accompanied by a good intention.

6. The somewhat disliked (*makrūh tanzīhan*) is that which we have been commanded to leave, even though it is not sinful. The one who leaves it is rewarded, and the one who does it acted suboptimally.

7. The prohibitively disliked (*makrūh tahrīman*) is that which we have been firmly commanded to leave through a text open to possibility of interpretation.

Denying such a command is misguidance but not disbelief. Performing such an action is sinful.

8. The forbidden (*harām*) is that which we have been firmly commanded to leave, through a decisively established text.

APPENDIX

FARD ACTS OF WUDU: PAGE 16

1. Washing the entire face (once).

Wash your face from the top of the forehead to the bottom of the chin in length, and from earlobe to earlobe in width.

2. Washing both arms (once).

Wash your hands and arms. This means all parts of your hands including between the fingers and up to and including the elbows.

3. Wiping a quarter of the head (once).

Wiping of the head should be done on the top of the head above ear level. If you were to make a circle around the top of your head just above your ears, any part of your head above the ears would be correct as long as it was a quarter of the head.

4. Washing both feet (once).

Washing the feet includes the ankles.

Concepts:
- Wiping and washing are not the same.

- Minimum wiping means to touch a limb with a wet hand.
- Washing means you are using enough water that one or two drops of water would fall.
- The head is the only part of the body that is wiped for *wudu*.
- Each limb being fully wet (without wasting water).

ACTIONS THAT BREAK WUDU: PAGE 18

1. When *najasa* (a physical impurity) exits the body.

Physical impurities: urine, feces, pus, flowing blood, and vomit of more than a mouthful (of other than phlegm and/or mucus). When these exit the body, it breaks our "state" of purity, therefore it breaks *wudu*.

Note: Anything that is considered impure that comes out of the private parts invalidates the ritual ablution as soon as it appears on the surface of the body. From other than the private parts, the ritual ablution is only invalidated if filth flows past its point of exit (such as a wound), or would have flowed had it not been wiped away.

Najasa is explained further in point 3 under "*Washing.*"

2. When air exits from the private parts.
- Air that exits from the private parts breaks our "state" of purity and therefore also breaks our *wudu*.

- In the case of females, air sometimes exits from the front passage of the private parts. This does not break *wudu*.

3. Laughing aloud (audibly) during prayer.
   - Laughing audibly is defined as being such that another person could hear the laughter.
   - Laughing audibly **during** prayer breaks *wudu* **and** *salah*.
   - Laughing such that only oneself can hear it invalidates the prayer, but does not break *wudu*.

Note1: Smiling doesn't break *wudu* or *salah*.

Note 2: Laughing at times other than *salah* does not break *wudu*.

4. Sleeping, lying down, or reclining on one's side.
   - Sleeping, lying down, or reclining on one's side breaks *wudu* because you are not aware if air has exited the private parts.
   - However, if one sleeps with one's buttocks firmly seated, one's ritual ablution is not invalidated.

WATER: PAGE 20
1. If one has limited water, one can still pray by performing the *fard* actions of *wudu*: (face, arms, head, feet).

2. If any portion of the *fard* limbs remains dry, the *wudu* is invalid.

3. One should always do a complete and perfect *wudu* with all the *sunnahs* except if one does not have enough water to do so, or the prayer time is running out.

Note 1: The *fard* actions only need to be performed once. To wash the limb 3 times is the *sunnah*, (except for the head which is wiped once regardless).

Note 2: If one does not have sufficient water to perform the *fard* actions, then one would do *tayammum*.

Note 3: Regardless of whether one does a complete and perfect *wudu* with all the *sunnahs* or only the *fard* of *wudu*, if any portion of a *fard* limb remains dry, the *wudu* is not valid.

WASHING: PAGE 22
1. When making *wudu* water must reach every part of the limb.

Pure water is to reach the complete outer skin. If the area of a pin hole remains in which water does not touch from the parts that are obligatory to wash, the *wudu* is not valid.

2. You must remove anything that prevents water from reaching the skin.

One must remove objects of dirt that prevent water from reaching the body such as wax or fatty grease: the same applies with nail polish, paint, or glue.

3. *Najasa* must be removed from your body, clothing or place of prayer before you pray.

A. *Najasa* or "filth" is divided into two types: heavy and light.
- Heavy filth includes: spilled or flowing blood, all intoxicating drinks, feces, urine of humans, urine of animals unlawful to eat (ex: fox, wolf), saliva of predatory animals (ex: dog), pus, vomit of more than a mouthful, droppings of non-flying birds that are permissible to eat (ex: turkey, chicken, swan, duck).
- Light filth includes: urine of animals permissible to eat (ex: sheep), urine of horses, droppings of flying birds impermissible to eat (ex: hawk, eagle, falcon).
- Not considered filth: droppings of flying birds permissible to eat (ex: pigeons).

B. How to remove *najasa*.
- A place with discernible filth (even if it is heavy) is purified by removing the filth itself even if this is achieved by washing it once. If its removal is difficult, there is no harm if some trace remains such as color or smell.

Note: However, if one can clearly see the flith has not been removed and will easily come off if you wash it once or twice more, it is allowed.

- A place with indiscernible filth on it is purified by washing and squeezing the area three times.

- Once you've washed and squeezed the item three times, consider it pure after that. There is no need to be doubtful.
- If it cannot be squeezed, it can be held under flowing water such that water strikes the area, leaves it, and is replaced with other water for a total of three times. If the fabric is delicate it can be be washed and then dried 3 times rather than squeezed. If an item cannot be squeezed, such as carpet, one can let it dry after each wash. Drying means for it to no longer drip. Complete drying is not a condition. Drying enough that one's hand would not get wet is sufficient. Also one may expedite the process by soaking the water up with a pure cloth (or vacuum suction) after each wash.

C. How much filth is excused?
- Regarding heavy filth, the size of a dirham is excused (about 3-5cm in diameter).
- Light filth which has afflicted less than one quarter of one's dress or body is excused.
- It is disliked to pray with even an excused amount of filth. One should not pray with this amount unless they fear they will miss the prayer time or prayer in congregation.

4. Having *najasa* on your body or clothing does **not** break *wudu*.

An example would be a baby urinating on you, a dog licking you, etc. In these cases you only wash the *najasa* before you pray. Your *wudu* is not broken.

- It is only when the *najasa* exits your body, blood, pus or urine for example, that your "state of purity" or *wudu* is broken.

5. Washroom essentials.

  A. Using the toilet.
  After using the toilet, ideally one should wipe clean the private parts with something dry (tissue), then wash to remove last traces of filth, then wipe to dry oneself.

  Note 1: It is a *fard* to have your body, clothes and place of prayer pure from *najasa* when you pray.

  Note 2: It is a *sunnah* to combine washing and wiping when cleaning oneself after using the toilet.

  Note 3: A wet tissue (or wet-wipe) alone does not fulfill the *sunnah*. Water must flow (flow = 1 or 2 drops drip off limb) for it to be considered washing.

  B. Slippers.
  Having slippers (for bathroom use only) helps keeps any traces of *najasa* from the bathroom off your feet so that you do not spread it throughout your home. This helps ensure your prayer area remains as pure as possible.

Note: It is *sunnah* to wear slippers when using the toilet.

FARD: CONDITIONS BEFORE PRAYER: PAGE 26

1. Knowing and believing that the prayer time has entered.

2. Being in a state of ritual purity (*wudu*).

3. One's body, clothes and place of prayer are free of filth (*najasa*) beyond the excused amount.

Note: See section on *najasa* for excused amount.

4. Clothing one's nakedness. For the female, it is her entire body except her hands (up to the wrist), feet (below the ankles) and face i.e., her wrist and ankle should be covered. For the male, it is from right below the navel to right below the knee.

5. Face the qiblah i.e. chest faces qiblah (direction of the *Ka'ba* in Makkah).

6. Make an intention before beginning the prayer.

Note 1: The place of intention is in the heart. There is no need to verbalize.

Note 2: There should be no undue interruption between the intention and the opening invocation (*takbir*, which is to say *Allahu Akbar*, "Allah is the greatest") by any action unrelated to the prayer.

If the prayer is superogatory, an unconditioned intention is sufficient; such as "I intend to pray." This also applies for emphasized *sunnah* prayers, though it is best to specify what one is praying: such as "I intend to pray the *sunnah* of *Maghrib*." The place of the intention is the heart; it is recommended to pronounce it when this helps one focus.

7. Pronouncing the opening invocation (*takbir*, saying *Allahu Akbar*). In the obligatory prayers this must be done standing, if one is able to stand without genuine hardship.

FARD: INTEGRALS WITHIN PRAYER: PAGE 28
1. Standing – for those able to stand, in obligatory prayers. The minimum standing position is such that if one were to extend one's arms they would not reach the knees.

2. Reciting at least one verse of Qur'an, whether long or short. It must be noted that it is prohibitively disliked (*makrūh tahrīman*) and sinful for the follower to recite behind the imām, both in loud and silent prayers.

Note: Thinking is not considered a valid recitation. The minimally valid recitation is to pronounce the letters by moving one's lips, even if no actual sound is made.

3. Bowing (*ruku'*), such that if one were to extend one's arms they would reach the knees.

4. Prostrating (*sujud*).

5. The final sitting, for the length of time it takes to recite the *tashahhud*.

Note: The final sitting is *fard*, the first sitting of a 3 or 4 *rak'ah* prayer is *wajib*.

WAJIB OF PRAYER (3 CATEGORIES): PAGES 30-37
The division of wajib into categories is uniquely the author's for ease of memorization and would not be found in traditional texts.

Significance of learning the *wajib*:
- If a *wajib* (necessary) action is left out due to forgetfulness, it can be made up by forgetfulness prostrations at the end of the prayer.

WAJIB: WHAT YOU SAY (WHAT YOU RECITE IN PRAYER): PAGE 30
Specific to the *fard* prayer:
1. Reciting the *Fatiha* (opening *surah* of the Qur'an) in the first 2 *rak'ah*.

2. Reciting another *surah* or (the equivalent of) three short verses in the first 2 *rak'ah*.

WAJIB: WHAT YOU SAY 2: PAGE 32

Specific to the *sunnah* or *Witr* prayers:
1. Reciting the *Fatiha* (opening *surah* of the Qur'an) in **every** *rak'ah*.

2. Reciting another *surah* or (the equivalent of) three short verses in **every** *rak'ah*.

In all prayers:
1. Reciting the *tashahhud* in the 2nd and final *rak'ah* (sometimes the 2nd *rak'ah* may also be the final *rak'ah*).

2. Saying *salām* twice at the end of the prayer (adding *'alaykum wa rahmatu 'Llah* is a confirmed *sunnah*, as is turning the head to the right for the first *salām*, and to the left for the second).

Although it is mentioned in this section of the poem, the following are emphasized *sunnah*, not *wajib*:
- If praying in congregation, to intend to greet the congregation, guardian angels and imām when making the closing *salāms*.
- If praying alone, to intend to greet only the angels in his finishing salāms.

WAJIB: HOW YOU RECITE: PAGE 34

Wajib for the imām only:
- For the *fard* of *Fajr*, and first 2 *rak'ahs* of *Maghrib* and *'Isha* prayers, he must recite Qur'an aloud.

Tip to help remember: the night/dark prayers are aloud.

Wajib for the followers behind the imām:
1. To **not** recite Qur'an whether the prayer is aloud or silent.

2. The follower recites everything except the Qur'an (they will recite the *dhikr, tashahhud, salām, "amīn", tasbihat*, etc.).

For the one praying alone:
1. Girls would recite quietly.

Note: It would be fine for a sister to raise her voice a little when praying the loud prayers alone, but not such that non-*mahram* men would hear her recital.

2. Boys have a choice to recite aloud or quietly for the night/dark prayers, the same prayers the imām would recite aloud: *Fajr, Maghrib & 'Isha* (first 2 *rak'ahs*). The rest of the prayers (daytime) would be recited quietly (*Dhuhr/'Asr*).

Concepts:
- Reminder: Thinking is not considered a valid recitation. The minimally valid recitation is to pronounce the letters by moving one's lips, even if no actual sound is made.
- Recitation is *fard*.
- Reciting quietly means to read in a voice you can hear yourself.

- Reciting aloud means it is loud enough that one praying beside you would hear it.
- A girl's reward is increased when she prays at home.
- A boy's reward is increased when praying at the *masjid*.

WAJIB: POSTURES OF PRAYER: PAGE 36

1. Making 2 successive prostrations in each *rak'ah*.

2. To remain motionless between prostrations for at least a moment.

3. To remain motionless when you stand after bowing for at least a moment.

4. Sitting after 2 *rak'ah* for a 3 or 4 *rak'ah* prayer.

Note: Sitting after 2 *rak'ah* for a 3 or 4 *rak'ah* prayer is *wajib*, the final sitting is *fard* (for every prayer).

5. To sit as long as it would take you to recite the *tashahhud*.

PROSTRATION OF FORGETFULNESS: PAGE 38

1. The prostration of forgetfulness is performed in the final sitting.

2. One sits at the final sitting and recites the *tashahhud*.

3. One then turns their head to the right only (for the *salām*) and says *"Assalamu 'alaykum wa rahmatu 'Llah"*.

4. Then prostrates twice exactly as he would do in any prayer saying the *takbir (Allahu Akbar)* and *tasbih (subhana Rabial 'Aala)*.

5. After the two prostrations the individual remains sitting.

6. He then recites *tashahhud* as if he just sat for the last sitting.

7. He would then continue to pray as he would normally at the last sitting, saying the *durood (ibrahimiya)*, *du'a*, and conclude with finishing *salām*.

ACTIONS THAT BREAK THE PRAYER: PAGE 40

1. Any excessive movement will break the prayer. Excessive movements, which invalidate the prayer are those that would make an onlooker who is unaware that the person is praying, think they are not in prayer.

2. Speaking anything other than that of prayer such as returning a greeting.

3. Eating or pulling something from the teeth larger than a chickpea.

4. Moaning (by saying "Ah", or the like) unless it is out of unbearable pain.

5. Crying for worldly reasons (such as sadness due to worldly concerns). If it is out of remembrance of the afterlife, or on a reflection of a verse of the Qur'an being recited, it does not break the prayer.

6. Coughing without need. Need would include clearing one's throat or improving one's ability to recite or supplicate.

7. Moving your chest completely away from the direction of the qiblah without necessity.

REFERENCES

The Absolute Essentials of Islam, compiled by Shaykh Faraz Fareed Rabbani, based on Shaykh Amin Jundi's *Islah 'Ilm al-Hal*

Ascent to Felicity, by Abu 'l-Ikhlas al-Shurunbulali, Translation, Notes, and Appendices by Faraz A. Khan

Nur al Idah, Hasan Shurunbulali, translated from the Arabic with commentary and notes by Wesam Charkawi

Seeker's Hub Answers: http://seekershub.org/ans-blog

GLOSSARY OF ARABIC TERMS

SACRED RULINGS

Hanafi Madhhab: school of law founded by Imām Abu Hanifa

fiqh: rulings of sacred law

PRAYER TIMES

Fajr: from entrance of true dawn to right before sunrise

Dhuhr: immediately after mid-day until the shadow of an object is

    (a) 1st opinion: twice its own length or

    (b) 2nd opinion: equal to its own length

'Asr: begins immediately after *Dhuhr* until right before sunset

Maghrib: sunset until disappearance of red twilight

'Isha & Witr: right before disappearance of red twilight to right before *Fajr*

PRAYER POSTURES

jalsa: sitting

qiyam: standing

rak'ah: one unit of prayer

ruku': bowing

sajda: prostrating

taslim: saying "*salām*" while turning your head to the right and left at the end of prayer

PRAYER RECITATIONS

Al Fatiha: the first chapter of the Holy Qur'an

Allahu Akbar: God is the Greatest

durood: recited in sitting position, begins with "*Allahumma salli ala Muhammad wa 'ala ali Muhammad*"

Qur'an: the final revelation of God

salām: exiting prayer with "*Assalaamu 'alaykum wa rahmatullah*"

surah: a chapter of the Qur'an

takbir: to praise God by saying "*Allahu Akbar*"

tashahhud: recited in sitting position, begins with "*At tahiyyatu li'llahi wa salawatu wa tayyibat(tu)*"

PRAISE

Alhamdulillah: all thanks and praise be to God

Masha Allah: as God wills

OTHER TERMS

'alim/'alimah: male/female scholar of sacred sciences

Allah: God

dirham: silver coin 3-5 cm in size

du'a: supplication

imām: prayer leader

nabi: prophet

najasa: filth

qiblah: direction of prayer

rasool: messenger

salah: ritual prayer

Witr: 3 units of prayer after *'Isha*

FIQH TEACHERS

Born and raised in Northern California, **Shamira Chothia Ahmed** is an emerging female scholar of the traditional Islamic sciences. Her studies led her to seek sacred knowledge from scholars on three continents — Africa, Europe, and Asia. In England she completed the five-year, traditional *'alimah* (Islamic studies) program, studied the ahadith collection of the Sihah Sittah and received her *ijaazah* (authorization) in Sahih al-Bukhari with renowned Hanafi scholars. Thereafter, Shamira was able to continue her studies for six months in Damascus, Syria where she obtained an *ijaazah* in *tajwid* of the Hafs recitation from the late eminent Syrian scholar, Shaykh Abu Hassan al-Kurdi. Upon returning to the U.S. in 2005, she was granted the opportunity to be an instructor of Hanafi *fiqh* for women at the Zaytuna Institute in Hayward, California. Privately, she taught *fiqh*, *tajwid* and Qur'anic *tafsir* (exegesis).

In 2008 Shamira earned her Master's degree in Demographics and Social Analysis from the University of California at Irvine with her focus on the identity formation of the Muslim-American population. She is one of the co-founders of the Rahmah Foundation, which is a U.S. sisters' organization dedicated to teaching women their fardh al 'ayn knowledge by qualified female scholars. Her latest endeavors include her popular "Blessed Birthings" seminar on natural childbirth in Islam, and "Nursing Your Baby Naturally", a course based on her qualification as a certified lactation educator/counselor.

Shamira specialized in the detailed rulings of menstruation, lochia, and abnormal discharge under the direction of Mufti Abdur Rahman Ibn Yusuf Mangera.

Shamira is both a wife and mother of four young children. She enjoys giving interactive and uplifting talks to sisters across the U.S.

Imam Tahir Anwar is an American Muslim scholar and preacher. Born in London, England, he has lived in the San Francisco Bay Area since 1983.

After completing his religious studies, Imam Tahir has served the Bay Area Muslim community since 2000. He also teaches Islamic Law at the renowned Zaytuna College, America's first Muslim liberal arts college located in Berkeley, CA.

In addition, he is the founding board member of Averroes High School, the Bay Area's first Muslim high school. He is currently the chairman of the board of NISA, North-American Islamic Shelter for the Abused, an organization that works towards alleviating issues related to domestic violence.

He has a passion for community service. He served on the Human Rights Commission for the City of San Jose for over 5 years and on the Human Relations Commission for the County of Santa Clara for one year. He also leads a group for Hajj each year.

AUTHOR

Ameena is an American-Muslim born and raised in Northern California. She is the youngest of five children and has a bachelor of science degree in Computer Science. Her connection to poetry and spirituality was ignited as a young girl when she first read poems about God and His Messenger ﷺ in the preface of *The Elementary Teachings of Islam*. They touched her heart. During her years as a Sunday school student, Ameena continued to write basic rhymes related to her faith. After becoming a mother, she began studying Islam formally and once again started writing, beginning with a poem she titled "My Way Back."

Ameena has benefited from amazing scholars at Zaytuna Institute (before Zaytuna College) such as Imam Tahir Anwar, Ustadha Shamira Chothia Ahmed, Shaykh Yahya Rhodus, Ustadha Saira Abu Bakr, Imam Zaid Shakir, and Shaykh Hamza Yusuf. After she studied Hanafi *Fiqh*, Ameena was given permission to teach. She has taught women and children privately in homes, Sunday schools, and local mosques. Ameena also opened her home often for learning in a fun way. Children have done Islamic crafts on her dining table, learned *fiqh* in her living room, and made *wudu* on her lawn. Ameena has a great love for nature and her favorite place is the ocean. In her spare time she loves learning, writing and reflecting on the signs of God.

ILLUSTRATOR

Reyhana Ismail is a UK-based graphic designer and illustrator. Although much of her career was spent as the Design Director of SISTERS magazine, her work has evolved into book design and illustration. *Purity and Prayer* was her first fully illustrated children's book, for which she will always be thankful to Allah ﷻ, and to Sr Ameena for having the confidence in her with this amazing project. Whilst *Purity and Prayer* was created digitally, she has since begun to explore hand-drawn illustration, going back to basics with pencils and paper - and rediscovering a passion for her work in the process.

In her personal life, Reyhana is a married mother of two, with whom she loves to bake, read and draw. She dreams of spending every summer in her favourite village in Turkey.

Her online store sells a range of beautifully designed yet functional stationery, from Ramadan planners to annual diaries.
Visit her website at www.reyoflightdesign.com.

الحمد لله رب العالمين

www.ingramcontent.com/pod-product-compliance
Lightning Source LLC
Chambersburg PA
CBHW040453100426

42813CB00022BA/2991